The Little Book of

ANIMALS OF THE RAINFOREST

**BUSHEL
& PECK
BOOKS**

Published by Bushel & Peck Books, www.bushelandpeckbooks.com.

Bushel & Peck Books is dedicated to fighting illiteracy all over the world.
For every book we sell, we donate one to a child in need——book for book.
To nominate a school or organization to receive free books,
please visit www.bushelandpeckbooks.com.

Type set in Temeraire, Avenir Next, and Bebas.

Illustrations sourced from the Biodiversity Heritage Library. Other image credits as follows:
vine pattern: Nespola Designs/Shutterstock.com; graph paper background: Vector Image
Plus/Shutterstock.com; cover monkey, jaguar, and title page macaw: The Graphics Fairy;
frog icon: Duiti Serizawa/Shutterstock.com.

Animal taxonomy sourced from Wikipedia.

ISBN: 9781638191452

First Edition

Printed in the United States

10 9 8 7 6 5 4 3 2 1

The Little Book of

ANIMALS OF THE RAINFOREST

CHRISTIN FARLEY

Contents

Crimson
Topaz
Hummingbird

Peruvian
Coquette
Hummingbird

BRAINY BIRDS

While expert at finding nectar, hummingbirds have another amazing trait— memory! These birds can remember every flower they've ever visited, not to mention their migration routes. Perhaps this is because their brains are proportionally the largest of any bird.

1. HUMMINGBIRD

"Iridescent" and "tireless" are words that can be used to describe the world's smallest birds. Known for their slight stature, hummingbirds are on the constant hunt for food while bringing beauty to the world around them. Whether migrating long distances or zipping around your backyard bird feeder, these birds can catch your eye with their darting movements and array of color. They are part of the Trochilidae family of avian birds and prefer to live solitary lives in the Western Hemisphere. Throughout history, hummingbirds have had significant importance to native cultures.

FANCY FLIERS

Amazingly agile, hummingbirds are dynamic flyers. These birds can fly backwards, upside down, or hover in the air indefinitely. They can do all this while flapping their wings at speeds of up to 80 beats per second.

BY THE NUMBERS

1,000–2,000	*the number of flowers visited each day*
300+	*known species of hummingbirds*
1,200	*the distance (in miles) a ruby-throated hummingbird can fly without stopping during migration*

Ruby-Throated Hummingbird

FIGHT OR FLIGHT?

If a macaw finds itself in a precarious situation, it will usually take flight. Its tail makes up half of its body length, so the macaw can turn around to provide a mouthful of feathers for its opponent. However, should a predator venture too close, a macaw can fight back with its curved beak and sharp talons.

2. SCARLET MACAW

Arguably the most beautiful member of the parrot family, the scarlet macaw is full of personality. Macaws maintain a long-term commitment to their mates and even have the intelligence to learn tricks and mimic speech, making them a highlight of the avian world. In their natural habitat of dense rainforests, scarlet macaws blend in easily with the vivid colors of plants and flowers. Bright red feathers cover their body and white skin encircles their eyes. Their wingtips are deep blue and yellow, giving them a majestic appearance. Due to the rapid loss of habitat from deforestation, humans are their number one source of danger.

CLASSIFICATION

KINGDOM: *Animalia*

PHYLUM: *Chordata*

CLASS: *Aves*

ORDER: *Psittaciformes*

FAMILY: *Psittacidae*

GENUS: *Ara*

SPECIES: *A. macao*

BY THE NUMBERS

2	the years a juvenile scarlet may stay with its family
60	average lifespan in years of a scarlet macaw
3	approximate wingspan in feet

DEPENDABLE DROPPINGS

Macaws have an important role to play in their local plant life. While nuts are a significant part of their diet, they are also avid fruit and berry eaters. Known as "seed bearer" species, macaw droppings are helpful in reseeding deforested areas as they are packed with fruit seeds.

GIRLS IN CHARGE

Female spider monkeys take the lead in their matriarchal troops. When breeding time comes, they will choose their own mates, cutting down on male aggressiveness toward each other.

Each troop also has an alpha female that will make decisions on feeding ground locations and the ultimate size of the group.

Variegated
Spider
Monkey

3. SPIDER MONKEY

Spider monkeys are one of the small primates that call the canopies of South and Central America home. They earn their name from the spider-like way they use their extra-long tails to hang from trees. Such tails are designed for arboreal life; they lack hair on the underside to help with grip, and their strength is like that of an extra limb. Spider monkeys also have a unique adaptation compared to other primates—no opposable thumbs. This makes their hand hook-like and enables them to grip branches more easily as they swing through trees. Like furry brown acrobats, spider monkeys will make you smile when they hang upside down to eat with both hands or swing themselves up to stand on a limb.

BY THE NUMBERS

3	approximate height in feet
30	distance they can travel in feet with one swoosh of their arms
35	length their tails can grow in inches (longer than their bodies!)

SLOW GROWTH

The slow reproductive rate of spider monkeys makes conservation efforts a challenge. Mothers only give birth to one baby every two to four years, and the gestation period lasts about seven months. The baby will not be weaned for 12-20 months, receiving lots of care and teaching from its mother.

Red-Faced Spider Monkey

LETHAL LEVELS

When it comes to the golden poison dart frog, you can look but don't touch! The most toxic of all the species, ingesting its poison can stop the human heart in almost an instant! Its toxins only amount to one milligram of poison, but that goes a long way. One frog can kill two African bull elephants or twenty humans.

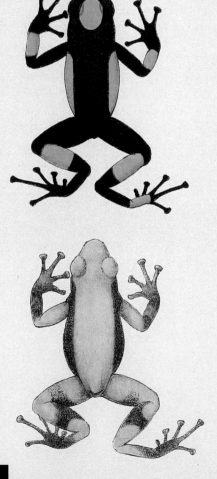

4. POISON DART FROG

The more bright and attractive the coloring, the more dangerous the poison dart frog is! Even from a distance, they are a wonder to behold with their many unique color patterns and variations, making the rainforest feel full of possibilities. Unlike a snake that releases venom through its fangs, these frogs release it through their skin and only in self-defense. As most predators have learned to keep their distance, the fire-bellied snake is the only natural predator of poison dart frogs. When they are not hunting for spiders and small insects, poison dart frogs can be found in small groups wrestling over egg-laying sites and territories.

BY THE NUMBERS

1	length in centimeters of the smallest frog
15	longest they can live in years
170+	species of poison dart frog

RESOURCEFUL RESIDENTS

Indigenous people of South America understand the power of the poison dart frogs. For centuries, they have rolled arrow tips and blow-darts over the skin of live frogs to coat them in poison. This makes it easier to hunt as the poison can paralyze an animal. Such weapons are also used against enemy tribes today!

MISTAKEN IDENTITY

Due to their color and markings, jaguars are often mistaken for leopards. One big difference is their spots, called "rosettes." On closer examination, jaguar rosettes are larger and contain spots in the middle that the leopard rosettes lack. Also, leopards are found in Asia and Africa, while jaguars hail from the Americas.

5. JAGUAR

While very speedy, jaguars can tire quickly; therefore, they can be found in trees ready to pounce on their unsuspecting prey. Unlike other cats, jaguars love the water and are capable swimmers. They've been known to feed on fish, turtles, caimans, and anacondas! Outside of mating season, jaguars live solitary lives, marking their territory by clawing trees and excreting waste. With the most powerful bite of the "big cats," the jaguar truly is "king of the jungle."

BY THE NUMBERS

250	*weight they can reach in pounds*
15	*lifespan in years in the wild*
50	*pounds of food they consume a day*

SACRED SYMBOL

Jaguars have played important roles in Central and South American cultures. They have influenced art, mythology, and religious practices. The ancient Aztec, Mayan, and Incan civilizations worshiped the jaguar and built temples in its honor. For them, the jaguar stood for ferocity, power, and valor.

FAMILY MATTERS

Male and female marmosets mate for life. Most commonly, a mated pair will have non-identical twins. The mothers' pregnancy lasts four to six months, and the fathers are both loyal and diligent caretakers to their young. While the mother recovers from giving birth, the father licks and grooms the new baby.

6. PYGMY MARMOSET

K nown as the smallest monkey in the world, the pygmy marmoset can fit in your hand. Their soft and silky hair of brownish-orange gives them an adorable appearance that compliments their small stature. Life for the pygmy marmoset is spent actively foraging in the treetops of South America in small troops. Here, marmosets feed on insects, fruit, and tree sap from one or two trees. This continues until sources are depleted, causing them to move to a new home range. Instead of nails, marmosets have claws that help them grip branches as they move through the treetops, limiting their visibility to predators. Such predators consist of pit vipers and cats like ocelots and margays.

CLASSIFICATION

KINGDOM: *Animalia*

PHYLUM: *Chordata*

CLASS: *Mammalia*

ORDER: *Primates*

SUBORDER: *Haplorhini*

INFRAORDER: *Simiiformes*

FAMILY: *Callitrichidae*

GENUS: *Cebuella*

SPECIES: *C. pygmaea*

BY THE NUMBERS

12	*lifespan in years in the wild*
3.5	*weight in ounces of an adult*
1	*size in acres of a troop's home range*

STRANGER DANGER

No one likes getting picked on, marmosets included. When predators come near, marmosets can attack in mob behavior with loud squeals and vocalizations until the threat is gone. An opposite (yet effective) tactic is for the group to stay completely still to avoid detection by an oncoming predator.

FAMILIAR FACES

Do capuchin monkeys look familiar to you? If so, it could be because they have starred in movies and television shows. Being highly intelligent and easy to train, these monkeys have made their mark in show business. In some countries, you can also find them (near their owner) doing street tricks and entertaining bystanders.

7. CAPUCHIN MONKEY

European explorers of South America gave the capuchin monkeys their name. The hooded, brown tufts of fur on their head resembled the brown-hooded robes of the Capuchin Friars within the Catholic Church. Also known as white-faced monkeys, capuchins typically live in the rainforest canopies of Honduras, Ecuador, and Columbia. Living an arboreal lifestyle, the monkeys are daytime foragers that feast on fruits, insects, and plant life. Capuchins are one of the most intelligent monkey species, second only to the spider monkeys. Resourceful, they are known to rub certain plants on their fur to repel mosquitos and are one of the only non-human primates to use tools for defense and hunting.

BY THE NUMBERS

35	*running speed in miles per hour*
1	*average litter size*
8	*approximate weight in pounds*

SOCIAL BEING

Life can appear carefree for the capuchin monkeys; they always seem to be smiling in their familial groups of up to 35. It's evident from their behavior that they enjoy social bonds. Some interesting ways to show their affection are by poking each other's eyes; sucking on the fingers, ears, and tails of another monkey; and even taking a bite out of another's tuft of fur.

LATE NIGHT CALLS

Squirrel monkeys are incredibly social and can congregate in troops of 300-500. While they are active in the daytime, they can still communicate with each other after nightfall. Even though they can't see each other in the darkness, they can differentiate between voices in the group and even have 25-30 vocal calls they make to each other.

8. SQUIRREL MONKEY

While not related to squirrels, squirrel monkeys get their name from their behavior. Excellent climbers, they spend their entire lives in the canopy treetops of the rainforest, running and leaping from branch to branch with agility and speed. Their long, spider-like fingers allow them to grip trees that provide coverage from predators like falcons and other birds of prey. Unlike other species, they don't have prehensile tails to swing from, using their tails only for balance. Though there are five main species of squirrel monkey, you can recognize the South American breed from its light gray fur, white face, and yellow legs.

BY THE NUMBERS

30	*length in inches (tail makes up over half the total length)*
25	*age in years they can reach*
2	*average weight in pounds of a male*

DID I JUST SEE THAT?

Your jaw might just drop when you see a squirrel monkey urinate on its own hands. Why would it do such a thing! It is part of a self-cleaning ritual and can help control their body temperature. Urine can also make their hands sticky, helping them to get a better grip on tree branches.

GIVING BACK

A plant-based diet is most common for peccaries. Unintentionally, they give back to the ecosystems around them by spitting out the large seeds of the plant they are eating while digesting the smaller seeds. The larger seeds will later sprout, reseeding the area.

Collared Peccary

9. PECCARY

Peccaries, also known as javelins, are easily mistaken for pigs and wild boars. With a dark, coarse coat and a cartilaginous snout, the confusion is understandable—that's not to mention their short, thin legs, large head, and barrel-shaped body! Some common differences are the stronger jaws and larger canines of the peccary. Areas of warm weather attract the peccary, such as the rainforests of South America and parts of Arizona in the United States. They can congregate in herds of 5-50, with the latter providing greater protection from predators like jaguars. Peccaries normally give birth to two babies who will learn to run within hours of birth!

BY THE NUMBERS

4	*greatest length they can reach in feet*
35	*top running speed in miles per hour*
60	*average weight of a peccary in pounds*

White-Lipped Peccary

COMMUNICATIVE CUES

Keen eyesight is not a natural trait of peccaries. To adapt, these social animals use smell and sound to communicate with each other. They can grunt, bark, or woof to pass on a message. They also show affection by grooming each other, laying close, and rubbing their bodies against one another.

DWINDLING DOWN

Brazilian tapir populations are on the descent, with only about 3,000 tapirs remaining. Both one of the largest land animals in Brazil and historically hunted, the tapir is considered endangered or vulnerable. Historically, tapirs were raised on farms for their meat and skin. More recently, however, conservation efforts have begun in hopes of keeping this species around indefinitely.

10. BRAZILIAN TAPIR

Fossils of the tapir have been found all over the world, giving rise to the belief that they've been around for millions of years. Today, however, tapirs only inhabit a few areas of the globe, one being the rainforests of Brazil. Their physical appearance resembles a combination of an elephant, a pig, and an anteater; this is thanks to their sturdy brown bodies, trunks, and short legs. Unlike other tapir species, the Brazilian tapir prefers to live alone near leaves, fruit, and other food sources, but they will follow the tracks of others to find water. Their trunk can be used as a snorkel, allowing them to stay submerged underwater for about three minutes.

CLASSIFICATION

KINGDOM: *Animalia*

PHYLUM: *Chordata*

CLASS: *Mammalia*

ORDER: *Perissodactyla*

FAMILY: *Tapiridae*

GENUS: *Tapirus*

SPECIES: *T. terrestris*

BY THE NUMBERS

700	weight they can reach in pounds
1	number of calves born a year to a female tapir
25	lifespan in years in the wild

WHERE TO MEET

So, you are interested in discovering more about Brazilian tapirs but not sure about trying to find one in the wild? No worries! There are plenty of zoos that house these interesting creatures to help you learn more. The San Diego Zoo (California), the Alexandria Zoo (Louisiana), and the Adelaide Zoo (Australia) are good places to start.

LOOKS CAN BE DECEIVING

While ocelots are adorable and soft, they are also highly territorial and hostile toward each other. Ocelots have no problem fighting each other if their territory is threatened. The only time they seem to tolerate each other is during mating season, after which the mother will raise her kittens on her own for up to two years.

11. OCELOT

Ocelots are carnivorous wild cats that are commonly found in areas of the rainforest with dense vegetation. Twice the size of house cats, ocelots earned the nickname "dwarf leopard" from their status as the second largest spotted cats in South America behind the jaguar. On their backs, ocelots have golden fur covered with black lines and spots, while on their underbellies, ocelots have white fur. Daytime is mostly spent relaxing in trees where they can remain hidden from predators like jaguars, anacondas, and harpy eagles. Nocturnal, ocelots hunt at night and are known to stalk their prey like monkeys and birds. Their success in hunting is aided by their amazing climbing, swimming, and jumping abilities.

BY THE NUMBERS

34	the weight in pounds an adult can reach
4	distance in miles a female will travel to hunt at night
2-3	average size of an ocelot litter

ARTIFACTS OF INTEREST

Ancient Aztec civilizations—along with other indigenous cultures of South America—held the ocelot in high regard. The word "ocelot" is believed to have come from the Aztec word "tlalocelot," meaning "field tiger." These cats have been depicted in ancient art and on jewelry and pottery for their beauty and hunting prowess.

SOLAR POWER

Cars and houses are not the only things that can run on solar power. Sloths rely on the sun's energy to regulate their body temperature. Sloths have the slowest digestion of any mammal, with one meal taking two weeks to digest. Their slow metabolism requires them to sunbathe to keep up their body temperature, similar to reptiles.

12. BROWN-THROATED SLOTH

Brown-throated sloths appear just as their name describes—they are covered with pale brown fur and sport darker brown shades on their foreheads and throats. Incredibly adorable, these sloths have round heads, small teeth, and always seem to be smiling! Known for their snail-like speed, the only thing unnerving about them is their long, sharp claws. Brown-throated sloths are herbivorous and, thankfully, use their claws for grabbing tree branches. But if they feel threatened, those three-to-four-inch-long claws can become weapons of destruction. Solitary animals, sloths will spend the majority of their lives in the treetops of Central and South America.

BY THE NUMBERS

18	hours a day they can spend sleeping
40	years they can live in the wild
300	degrees the sloth can turn its head (like an owl!)

WHEN YOU'VE GOTTA GO . . .

It's risky business for sloths to climb down from their trees. With slow and awkward movement on land, they become easy targets for predators like harpy eagles. Thankfully, they don't have to make the trek very often. One benefit of a slow metabolism is that they only have to descend from the canopy once a week to defecate and urinate.

One of the identifying characteristics of a puma is its uniformly tan-colored fur. On the other hand, puma cubs are born with black spots on their golden-red fur. While they might resemble cubs of a jaguar, the spots help the puma cubs camouflage in the dense forest, increasing their chance of survival.

13. PUMA

Pumas are the largest of the small cat species, though you might know them as cougars or mountain lions. The word "puma" means "cat of one color" since they don't have any markings on their fur like leopards and jaguars. Erect ears, round heads, and tan-colored coats are the identifying features of pumas. These adaptive cats can be found as north as the Yukon but are also prevalent in Amazon rainforest. While they can't roar like larger cats, pumas are known to purr, hiss, growl, and scream.

CLASSIFICATION

KINGDOM: *Animalia*

PHYLUM: *Chordata*

CLASS: *Mammalia*

ORDER: *Carnivora*

SUBORDER: *Feliformia*

FAMILY: *Felidae*

SUBFAMILY: *Felinae*

GENUS: *Puma*

SPECIES: *P. concolor*

BY THE NUMBERS

8	*length in feet a male puma can grow*
15	*height they can jump in feet*
160	*weight in pounds a male puma can reach*

CONSTANT COMPETITION

With no natural predators, you might think life must be pretty good for a puma. However, every animal faces its challenges. The biggest challenge for pumas is competition for food with other large mammals. In the rainforest, the jaguar is the fiercest competitor, and pumas can be injured or killed when confrontation occurs over a meal.

THE UNTHINKABLE

It's difficult to conceive of, but capybaras eat their own poop! "Autocoprophagous" is the term used for animals that eat their own feces, and they do this for added nutrition. A diet of grass is hard to digest, and eating their poop provides bacterial flora to aid proper digestion.

14. CAPYBARA

If you've ever seen a guinea pig, imagine one the size of a dog, and you have imagined a capybara! These semi-aquatic mammals thrive on land and in water as the world's largest rodent. Covered in brown fur, capybaras are found throughout South America and are surprisingly agile on their short legs. They can run from predators like pumas, caimans, and anacondas at speeds of over 20 mph. Another escape route is into nearby waters, where webbed feet give them a chance to show off their excellent swimming capabilities. They can remain underwater for five minutes and even sleep in the water with only their noses above the surface.

CLASSIFICATION

KINGDOM: *Animalia*

PHYLUM: *Chordata*

CLASS: *Mammalia*

ORDER: *Rodentia*

FAMILY: *Caviidae*

GENUS: *Hydrochoerus*

SPECIES: *H. hydrochaeris*

BY THE NUMBERS

201	*weight in pounds of the heaviest capybara ever!*
10	*lifespan in years in the wild*
8	*pounds of grass they can consume a day*

TIME TO CHILL

Capybaras are known as "nature's ottoman" because they provide a soft place to rest for many smaller animals. It is common for birds, monkeys, and rabbits to take a ride on a capybara. This service can be mutually beneficial as birds will eat pests out of the capybara's fur.

DYING OF THIRST

Common vampire bats drink about half their weight in blood each night. If they go two nights without finding enough blood, they will die. Thankfully, vampire bats are good at sharing, and another well-fed bat may regurgitate blood to share with those in need. In exchange for their life-saving meal, they expect grooming services from the receiver.

15. COMMON VAMPIRE BAT

W hile they do drink the blood of other animals, vampire bats are not as terrifying as their name sounds. Actually, human blood is not on their menu, and it has been found that they are quite tame and friendly around humans. Birds, horses, pigs, or even a sleeping cow are not as fortunate. Vampire bats prefer to feed on these animals, though they never take enough blood to harm them. Unfortunately, besides being annoying to animals, the bites can cause infection and disease. Being agile and light in weight, vampire bats can feed on an animal for 30 minutes without waking them from sleep, afterwards stealthily returning to their dark caves and hollow trees undetected.

BY THE NUMBERS

1	*weight in ounces*
200	*days to complete the gestation cycle*
7	*wingspan in inches*

SHARING IS CARING

There is plenty of competition when it comes to finding and keeping a host for a blood meal. Common vampire bats will fend off other bats who attempt to feed on their host. However, having excellent manners, they will allow mothers and their offspring to feed alongside them.

1/5.

REMARKABLE RELATIONS

Giant armadillos have a remarkable ancestor: a prehistoric giant armadillo named Doedicurus. It, too, lived in South America about 10,000 years ago with other Ice Age animals. Though it has been extinct for thousands of years, scientists believe it was also a herbivore that looked like armadillos of today. The biggest difference was its prehistoric size of 13 feet in length and weight of around 2,200 pounds.

16. GIANT ARMADILLO

Giant armadillos boast an impressive casing of plates and scales; these scales earned them their name from the Spanish word "armadillo," meaning "little armored one." Their armored tops are usually gray in color, but their undersides are wrinkly and pink. While they look formidable, giant armadillos are not very territorial. Instead of defending their home turf, they are more likely to walk away, continuing their solitary lives in the forests and savannas of South America. Their one true love is consuming the termites that they dig up in termite mounds with their large paws and sharp claws. An entire mound will only satisfy for one meal, so giant armadillos will also turn to worms, ants, and spiders on occasion.

CLASSIFICATION

KINGDOM: *Animalia*

PHYLUM: *Chordata*

CLASS: *Mammalia*

ORDER: *Cingulata*

FAMILY: *Chlamyphoridae*

SUBFAMILY: *Tolypeutinae*

GENUS: *Priodontes*

SPECIES: *P. maximus*

BY THE NUMBERS

72	*weight they can reach in pounds*
100	*greatest number of teeth an armadillo can have*
39	*length inches they can grow*

TODAY'S THREATS

The greatest threats to giant armadillos are not jaguars and pumas, but humans! Deforestation causes destruction to their habitats, and they are captured for resale in illegal trade. Giant armadillos also cause havoc for farmers, resulting in moves to hunt and eliminate them. These animals are considered pests, digging large burrows and causing damage to farms.

Hoatzin
(Young)

SOUNDS OF THE WILD

Communication is varied for hoatzins; they can make sounds like croaks, grunts, and hisses. When calling to another bird, hoatzins will make a series of low grunts, sometimes in a combination of three or more. If predators come near their chicks, hoatzins will make loud, wheezy, and raspy hissing noises to warn of danger.

17. HOATZIN

"**B**izarre" might be the best word to describe this noisy, clumsy, and smelly herbivorous bird. Found in the northern areas of South America, the hoatzin boasts a blue, featherless face with spiky orange feathers on its head, giving it the name "punk rock bird." This bird has a vibrant personality to match the variety of colors on its feathers. About the size of a pheasant, the hoatzin has underdeveloped chest muscles, making flight rare. Instead, they inhabit swamps and other bodies of water where they eat leaves and sunbathe on tree branches. Though not favored for their meat, hoatzins are highly regarded in Guyana as the national bird.

BY THE NUMBERS

25	*length in inches*
2	*approximate weight in pounds*
4	*hours a day spent eating*

STINK, STANK, STUNK

An unusual diet of marshy leaves gives the hoatzin its manure stench. Its "crop," or food storage pouch, breaks down food through a fermentation process like a cow. This process causes their unique odor that keeps local Amazonians from hunting them. Their stench saves their lives!

Male

BEAK POWER

King vultures don't actually hunt their prey. Instead, they spend hours gliding through air currents on the lookout for a potential meal. Since they lack a sense of smell, they rely on their powerful eyesight to locate carrion. With their strong, hooked beaks, they can tear open flesh more efficiently than other vultures.

Female

18. KING VULTURE

olumbia and Argentina are two common places to find a king vulture. The evergreen tropical forest canopies provide the needed protection against predators. While they are usually found alone, you can spot a vulture with its small, featherless head, orange beak, and red ring around its eyes. Its feathers are a robust white with black tips. And the fleshy orange bulge on its beak is called a "caruncle!" King vultures are helpful scavengers, ridding the rainforest of rotting animals with their taste for carrion. Their only natural enemies are snakes that prey on their young or eggs and the occasional jaguar which may not want to share its meal.

BY THE NUMBERS

10	weight they can reach in pounds
47	age in years of oldest known king vulture
5.5	wingspan length in feet

DIRTY AND CLEAN?

Eating the remains of dead animals sounds like a pretty dirty job. But just because they like a messy meal doesn't mean they like a messy appearance. King vultures are particular about their hygiene. They will travel long distances to wash themselves and will urinate on their own legs to kill bacteria and germs.

HOME DESIGNERS

Harpy nest building is a serious undertaking. First, nests are built over 90 feet in the air by lifelong mates. Construction materials consist of hundreds of branches and sticks mingled with animal fur and plants. Year after year, more material is added until they become large enough for an adult human to sleep comfortably inside!

19. HARPY EAGLE

Harpy eagles are large birds of prey with strong beaks and extraordinary flight capabilities— birds with these traits are commonly known as "raptors." One of the largest eagle species, the harpy is most common in Brazil's tropical lowland rainforests. With claws as strong as those of a grizzly bear and powerful, five-inch-long talons, harpy eagles are fierce predators. The primary coloring of a harpy eagle consists of a combination of white, black, and gray plumage. Their head feathers will stand up straight if in an alert state, giving them both an aggressive look and an interesting hairdo. Their facial disk feathers can also lift and lower to channel sound waves to their ears to improve hearing.

CLASSIFICATION

KINGDOM: *Animalia*

PHYLUM: *Chordata*

CLASS: *Aves*

ORDER: *Accipitriformes*

FAMILY: *Accipitridae*

SUBFAMILY: *Harpiinae*

GENUS: *Harpia*

SPECIES: *H. harpyja*

BY THE NUMBERS

1.75	*pounds of food they consume a day*
50	*flight speed they can reach in miles per hour*
20	*weight in pounds of a female (males weigh less)*

PATIENT FOR THE PREY

Even with their approximately 6.5-foot wingspan, harpy eagles are stealthy fliers as they glide through the jungle. If they want to conserve energy, they will perch for hours on a branch to wait for an unsuspecting animal to pass. With exceptional vision, they can see over 200 yards away, and they have the ability to grab animals up to 20 pounds in weight.

THANKS TO THE OWLS

Not only are they amazing creatures to look at, but spectacled owls also play an important role in their ecosystem. They aid in the population control of mammals and insects that could become unbalanced if they did not consume them. In addition, spectacled owls provide an important food source for larger predators.

20. SPECTACLED OWL

Spectacled owls are the largest and most dominant owls of the tropical forests and get their name from their appearance. White feathers around their eyes and throat make them look as though they are wearing glasses. While this gives them an adorable look when combined with their dark brown facial disk and yellow eyes, these owls are on the lookout for mice and insects on which to feast. Spectacled owls have an innate ability to hide undetected in trees, limiting their natural enemies. If they do have to defend themselves, they can ward off predators with their strong beaks and sharp talons. These adaptations keep spectacled owls on the "least concerned" species list.

BY THE NUMBERS

5	*years it can take for adults to obtain full plumage*
270	*degrees they can rotate their heads*
35	*lifespan in years in the wild*

ROUGH START

The clutch size of a spectacled owl is usually one to two eggs which hatch after a five-week incubation. Unfortunately, usually only one of these chicks will survive. Whichever chick is younger or smaller will die due to starvation or be killed by the older sibling.

THE MYSTERY CONTINUES

While a highly aggressive fish, much of what we know about payaras is still a mystery. Not enough research has been done to answer questions about their natural migration and reproduction. Will you be the next scientist to uncover the amazing traits of this fearsome fish?

21. PAYARA (VAMPIRE FISH)

The first thing you will notice when you see a payara is its TEETH! The nicknames "vampire fish," "Dracula fish," and "saber-toothed tiger fish" should no longer be a wonder. Payaras of the Amazon basin of South America have two elongated fangs and smaller, sharp, dagger-like teeth along their gums. Agile and fast swimmers, payaras live in fresh, fast-moving waters of streams and rivers. They are constantly on the hunt for their next meal of piranhas or other small-to-medium-sized fish.

BY THE NUMBERS

35	*weight they can reach in pounds*
3	*length in feet they can reach in the wild*
1	*maximum lifespan in years*

INTIMIDATION FACTOR

It's safe to say that payaras are moody fish who don't play well with other fish, preferring a solitary life. Other carnivorous fish like piranhas will try to stay away. To hunt, vampire fish will cause a panic as they dart into a school of fish. The frenzy makes it easier to spear a frightened fish.

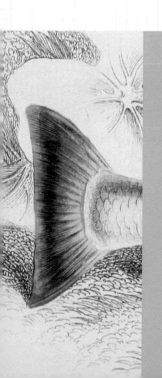

SHELL SPECIFICATIONS

The shell of a yellow-footed tortoise is most fascinating! Not only is it heavy and thick, but it is made up of 60 different bones all connected to each other! The coloring is usually a yellowish brown with possible black on the edges.

22. YELLOW-FOOTED TORTOISE

Yellow-footed tortoises get their name from—you guessed it—the yellow scales on their front legs! These large tortoises can reach 2.5 feet in length and enjoy the plants, fruits, and grasses of the South American rainforest. Occasionally, they may feed on the only animals they can catch—worms or snails! Mating occurs year-round, and male and female tortoises look almost identical. A male can tell a female apart from head movement. If a male and female encounter each other and there is no responsive head movement on her part, he assumes she is a female. After a 200-day incubation period, baby tortoises are born and are left to fend for themselves.

BY THE NUMBERS

35	*weight in pounds females can reach (the largest of the species are usually female)*
8	*largest clutch size*
50+	*lifespan in years*

HARM FROM HUMANS

While not on the endangered species list yet, the yellow-footed tortoise could be in the future. Their biggest threat is over-hunting by humans. They are caught and shipped to areas in South America where they are considered a culinary delicacy. Oil exploration, logging, and agriculture have also caused a loss of habitat for the tortoises.

HOW DOES IT DO THAT?

Running on water—now that is amazing! Basilisks can run on water at speeds of up to 15 mph for short distances. By paddling their hind legs very fast, they create pockets of air that keep them atop the water. For a human to do something like this, they would have to maintain a speed of 65 mph!

23. GREEN BASILISK

The basilisk is a Central American lizard that is also known as the "Jesus Christ lizard" due to its ability to walk on water (referencing the Biblical event). With bright green coloring and a fringe on its back, the basilisk looks like a miniature dinosaur! Home base is found 60+ feet above the ground in the trees of the rainforest, where they sunbathe during the day and are never far from a body of water. Here, they can feast on aquatic larvae, insects, and other reptiles. The dense foliage helps to evade predators, though they must stay vigilant against their number one nemesis—the quetzal bird.

BY THE NUMBERS

5	*feet per second in running speed*
2.5	*feet they can reach in length*
17	*eggs a female can lay during breeding season*

PERFECT PETS?

Both attractive and captivating, the green basilisk can make a great family pet. They are usually inexpensive, but parents should be aware that basilisks are skittish in nature and frighten easily. They also need a temperature-controlled enclosure with clean bedding and natural-looking decorations to climb on.

JAW-DROPPING

The diet of a red-tailed boa consists of monkeys, iguanas, birds, and rodents. How, you might wonder, is a boa able to consume an animal bigger than its head? A loosely hinged jaw is the key! Their stretchy jaw ligaments allow them to gape open their jaws to a width greater than the diameter of their heads.

24. RED-TAILED BOA

Preferring warm, humid weather, red-tailed boas find their perfect habitat in the semi-arid forests and tropical rainforests of Mexico and Central America. Though they will forage in trees at night, these nocturnal snakes tend to live in burrows and hollow logs and will cool off in rivers. You can spot red-tailed boas from their tan scales and around 20 dark dorsal saddles that run the length of their bodies. Their tails are usually blotched with red or black edging, and their yellowish bellies have black spots. Known for their size, these boas can grow to be 14 feet long and weigh around 30 pounds.

BY THE NUMBERS

2	length in feet at birth
2	weight in ounces at birth (same as two pencils!)
30	average lifespan in years in the wild

HOUSE PETS

How many parents would like to have a ten-foot snake cruising around the house? In some parts of Columbia and South America, families keep red-tailed boas as pets to kill rats, helping to control the rodent population! Thankfully, these non-venomous snakes are usually harmless to humans.

Common
Bottlenose
Dolphin

MAGICAL MYTHS

South American legends surround the pink river dolphin. One tale claims that, while swimming alone, the dolphins will whisk you away to a magical underwater city. Another story tells of pink river dolphins who morph into handsome men at night and visit local villages.

Amazon
Pink River
Dolphin

25. AMAZON PINK RIVER DOLPHIN

The Amazon pink river dolphin is both friendly and fascinating. Known for their coloring, they start off gray and slowly turn pink as they age. Exposure to sunlight, diet, and capillary placement influences their final coloration. Of the toothed whales, the pink river dolphin is the most diverse hunter, hunting 53 different animal species, including piranhas. They are also the only toothed whales to have two different types of teeth. The teeth in the back of the jaw are designed for crushing, while the front teeth are pointed. On top of all of this, Amazonian pink river dolphins have few natural predators; only occasionally do they become a meal for jaguars, caimans, or anacondas.

BY THE NUMBERS

8	*length they can reach in feet*
400	*weight in pounds*
180	*degrees they can turn their necks*

HUMAN HABITS

Pink river dolphins are shy creatures. Interestingly, when they are excited, they will blush bright pink, making them human-like! Speaking of humans, pink river dolphins have 40% more brain capacity than humans, giving them the largest brains of freshwater dolphins.

Keel-Billed
Toucan

WHO KNEW?!

A little-known fact about toucans is that they are related to the woodpecker family. Furthermore, their beaks are surprisingly soft, making it a useless tool for self-defense. Toucans are the national bird of Belize and are different from other bird species in that they sing louder in the daytime than the morning or night.

26. TOUCAN

Even though they are found in the rainforests of South and Central America, toucans are famous worldwide. Their characteristic black feathers and white neck compliment the blazing colors of their gorgeous beak! Across the 40 toucan species, there are many color combinations. While the beak gives toucans their signature look, this large appendage also makes reaching and peeling fruit easy. Additionally, toucans are able to regulate their body temperature by adjusting the amount of blood flow to their beaks. More blood flow creates greater warmth. Toucans have thriving social lives and can be found coexisting with various bird species in the trees, preferring to hop from place to place instead of flying.

CLASSIFICATION

KINGDOM: *Animalia*

PHYLUM: *Chordata*

CLASS: *Aves*

ORDER: *Piciformes*

INFRAORDER: *Ramphastides*

FAMILY: *Ramphastidae*

BY THE NUMBERS

5	greatest number of eggs they can lay at a time
20	average lifespan in years
6	length of its tongue in inches (and it looks like a feather!)

BEAK BY THE NUMBERS

Toucan beaks are about a third of the bird's total length, or about eight inches long. Compared to its body size, toucans have the largest beak of any bird. Thankfully, toucan beaks are much lighter than they look, averaging less than a pound and composed of the protein keratin.

White-Throated Toucan

FLOWER POWER

Only about 10% of a kinkajou's omnivorous diet comes from flowers and other plants. However, this habit is very beneficial to the local plant life. As kinkajous travel from flower-to-flower drinking nectar, the pollen sticks to their faces, allowing them to serve as important pollinators.

27. KINKAJOU

Kinkajous look similar to primates like monkeys. They even have similar prehensile tails that function as another limb, allowing them to move easily through the closed canopies of the rainforest. However, they are not closely related! Instead, they are related to (and about the same size as) raccoons. Kinkajous are covered in soft, brown fur and have small, round faces with large eyes. They excel at arboreal life and rarely leave the treetops. Sharp claws and fully reversible hind feet make them agile and acrobatic climbers. Occasionally, they can be seen in small groups eating with one another and grooming each other, though more often they are found to live on their own. Mating takes place year round, leading to the birth to one or two babies.

BY THE NUMBERS

90	*the percent of their diet that comes from fruit*
10	*weight in pounds they can reach*
22	*length they can reach in inches*

NOCTURNAL NAPPERS

Naturally nocturnal, kinkajous are rarely seen by people as they hide from light in tree holes and sleep during the daytime. Perhaps that is why they are called "night walkers" in Belize. They are hunted by diurnal birds (active day hunters) that will snatch a sleeping kinkajou from treetops, as well as foxes and ocelots.

PERSONAL HYGIENE

Just because they live in the wild doesn't mean siamangs have to look like it. An important social activity for them is grooming, and they spend a great deal of time grooming each other. Males will help to groom their young and spend an average of 15 minutes a day on their own appearance.

28. SIAMANG

Tall trees in the rainforests of Indonesia, Thailand, and Malaysia are where you are most likely to find a siamang. While they look similar to monkeys and live an arboreal life, the main difference is that they have two fingers that are fused together on each hand. They are the darkest and largest of the lesser apes (called "gobbins") and have a small patch of gray fur on their faces. Siamangs do not have tails, but they are still acrobatic athletes as they use their opposable thumbs to swing their slender, furry bodies from branch to branch. Their favorite foods are leaves and fruit, but they are known to consume bird eggs and insects.

KINGDOM: *Animalia*

PHYLUM: *Chordata*

CLASS: *Mammalia*

ORDER: *Primates*

SUBORDER: *Haplorhini*

INFRAORDER: *Simiiformes*

FAMILY: *Hylobatidae*

GENUS: *Symphalangus*

SPECIES: *S. syndactylus*

SWEET SONGS

Male and female siamangs mate for life and, as such, deepen their bond through song. In fact, a pair will fabricate a unique song just for them. Their special throat sacs amplify their songs to distances of up to two miles in the rainforest.

BY THE NUMBERS

8	*age at which they reach adulthood*
50	*size of territory in acres*
26	*weight they can reach in pounds*

POOP FROM THE GROUP

Fruits and berries are the foods of choice for cassowaries. Along with the occasional dead animal or fungi meal, a cassowary can consume up to 11 pounds of fruit a day. Fruit is usually only half-digested, leaving a partial meal behind after a cassowary defecates. Therefore, cassowaries don't mind eating their own poop and that of their neighbors!

29. CASSOWARY

Queensland, Australia is home to the world's most dangerous bird—the cassowary. Also the world's third largest bird, it can grow up to six feet in height and weigh over 100 pounds in Australia's unique tropical rainforest. Their appearance resembles a cross between a turkey and ostrich, but cassowaries are descendants of dinosaurs! Their backs are typically covered in black feathers, and they have blue upper legs. Cassowaries cannot fly, but they make up for their lack of flight with their running speed of up to 31 mph. They also excel at swimming and exhibit exceptional visual and auditory capabilities. Habitat loss is the main threat to the cassowary population.

BY THE NUMBERS

7	*height in feet they can jump off the ground*
50	*incubation period in days*
2	*verified reports of fatal cassowary attacks on humans*

FIT TO FIGHT

"Unpredictable" is an accurate description of a cassowary. While they are reclusive creatures, they have been known to attack for no reason. In fact, they attack over 200 humans a year with their powerful kicks. Victims are usually people who have ventured too close in hopes of feeding these beautiful birds.

FEEDING FRENZY

Anteaters are ant connoisseurs and can identify a particular ant or termite species before they even rip open the mound. Their highly developed sense of smell makes them forceful predators as they uncover nests with their powerful claws. Sticky saliva coats their lengthy tongue, enabling giant anteaters to consume about 30,000 insects per day.

30. GIANT ANTEATER

What mammal has a two-foot-long tongue, a petite head, a long snout, and no teeth? You guessed it—a giant anteater! Curious-looking creatures, giant anteaters have claws and back feet similar to that of a bear and bristly hair like that of a horse. Insect bites are no match for their thick skin and long hair. Generally solitary creatures, the anteater roams with a slow and shuffled gait through the tropical forests of Central and South America. Giant anteaters are also nomadic; they don't make permanent resting stops or nests but wander through their range of about one square mile in search of food.

BY THE NUMBERS

8	*length they can reach in feet*
100	*weight they can reach in pounds*
150	*the number of times they can flick their tongue in and out per minute*

MOTHER'S LOVE

A female giant anteater has a full time job. She raises a single pup by herself after a six-month-long pregnancy. After birth, the pup will nurse for six months and ride on her back for a year. Sometimes, the pup will be groomed by its mother for up to an hour at a time.

HELPFUL HORN

One of the most noticeable features of rhinoceros beetles is the curved horn atop their heads. It serves as a tool for males to drive other males away during mating rituals. The horn also allows the beetles to dig into the soil and leaf litter to escape dangerous predators.

31. RHINOCEROS BEETLE

One of the largest beetle species, rhinoceros beetles appear intimidating with their thick, armor-like exoskeleton and horn-like projection on their heads. Also known as the Hercules beetle, they can come in gray, black, or green coloring. Rhinoceros beetles have a wide range of dispersion; the rainforest is one of their many chosen habitats. With plenty of tree sap, vegetation, and rotting wood, these beetles thrive in moist climates. If you happen to come upon a rhinoceros beetle in the wild, you have no need to fear. Unable to bite or sting, they have a docile temperament and are even popular pets in parts of the world.

CLASSIFICATION

KINGDOM: *Animalia*

PHYLUM: *Arthropoda*

CLASS: *Insecta*

ORDER: *Coleoptera*

FAMILY: *Scarabaeidae*

SUBFAMILY: *Dynastinae*

TRIBE: *Oryctini*

BY THE NUMBERS

6	*length they can reach in inches*
8	*fastest recorded speed in miles per hour*
50	*number of eggs a female can lay*

BODYBUILDERS

The nickname "Hercules beetle" aptly describes the strength of the rhinoceros beetle. It's almost inconceivable to imagine it lifting 850 times its own weight. That would be comparable to an average human lifting over 14 Asian elephants!

FEAR FACTOR

It's a well-known fact that piranhas are naturally aggressive. However, exaggerated details have characterized them as river-dwelling, man-eating monsters. Scientists have debunked this myth. Attacks on humans can cause significant injuries, but piranhas don't actually eat humans unless they are deeply wounded or if the humans are already dead.

32. REDEYE PIRANHA

Just as you might imagine, redeye piranhas are ferocious hunters, each containing a set of bone-slicing teeth. Their diet consists of pieces of fin that have been nibbled off a variety of larger fish, but also fruits and plants that fall in the water. Living in the freshwater river basins of South America, redeye piranhas usually dwell alone, an interesting different from other piranhas who hunt in schools of 20-30 called "shoals." Their physical appearance is convex in shape, and their eyes are deep red (hence the name). Their bodies are thick and equipped with powerful tails that make for speedy swimming. The redeye piranha's natural predators include herons, crocodiles, and Amazon river dolphins.

KINGDOM: *Animalia*

PHYLUM: *Chordata*

CLASS: *Actinopterygii*

ORDER: *Characiformes*

FAMILY: *Serrasalmidae*

GENUS: *Serrasalmus*

SPECIES: *S. rhombeus*

BY THE NUMBERS

20	*average speed in miles per hour*
10	*normal lifespan in years*
20	*length they can reach in inches*

DINNER TIME!

It may surprise you, but red piranhas are edible to humans. In Brazil's Pantanal region, piranhas are grilled on banana leaves and even eaten in soups. Indigenous people of the Amazon are the common consumers of piranhas, along with caimans and river dolphins.

Paradise tanagers are successfully kept as household pets for many people. For proper care, they need plenty of water and a large cage. When it comes to their diet, you might have more in common with these birds than you realize. Are you a fan of tropical fruits and nuts? Do you like pears, bananas, and orange slices? Good news! These foods are adored by tanagers!

33. PARADISE TANAGER

Some of the world's most fascinating birds live in the Amazon rainforest. The paradise tanager is no exception! Its bright green head, black back feathers, beady eyes, blue chin, and blue belly make the tanager truly stunning! Paradise tanagers are medium-sized songbirds found in the subtropic and tropic forests of the Amazon basin. They tend to travel in small flocks of 10-15 and, occasionally, with other bird species. Foraging is a favorite pastime of the paradise tanager as they seek out insects on the underside of branches in the canopies of trees. While insects make for a tasty meal, tanagers also consume nectar, fruit, and berries.

LOOKALIKES

Male and female paradise tanagers are visibly identical. Sometimes, the only way to tell them apart is to test their DNA. One sure way to spot a female is when she deposits her two white-speckled eggs in her cup-shaped nest.

CLASSIFICATION

KINGDOM: *Animalia*

PHYLUM: *Chordata*

CLASS: *Aves*

ORDER: *Passeriformes*

FAMILY: *Thraupidae*

GENUS: *Tangara*

SPECIES: *T. chilensis*

BY THE NUMBERS

5	*length in inches*
.6	*weight in ounces*
16	*incubation period in days*

TRUE BLUE?

The wings of the blue morpho butterfly are not actually blue at all! They owe their blue appearance to the way light reflects off their wings' microscopic scales. This type of optical illusion is known as "iridescence," and only the male blue morphos appear blue!

34. BLUE MORPHO BUTTERFLY

Life begins for the blue morpho butterfly once it hatches from its pale green egg. From there, it progresses from a larva to a brown, hairy caterpillar with colorful patches on its back. Though aesthetically striking, nothing compares to the blue beauty that emerges after 14 days in its chrysalis! In addition to being lovely to look at, the blue morpho is also known for its behavioral adaptations. For protection, the butterflies feed on poisonous plants, making them an unwanted food source for predators. Their diet also consists of rotting foods and tree sap, which are plentiful in rainforests. This allows them to have consistent and easy-to-find food sources.

CLASSIFICATION

KINGDOM: *Animalia*

PHYLUM: *Arthropoda*

CLASS: *Insecta*

ORDER: *Lepidoptera*

FAMILY: *Nymphalidae*

GENUS: *Morpho*

SPECIES: *M. menelaus*

BY THE NUMBERS

29	*total number of morpho butterfly species*
8	*wingspan in inches*
115	*average lifespan in days*

INTERESTING APPEAL

Scientists have been fascinated by the light-reflecting abilities of butterflies like the blue morpho. This phenomenon has aided and inspired human technology. The same technique is being used on money that includes iridescent strips to prevent counterfeit bills.

TERRIFIC TONGUES

Okapi tongues are fascinating! Scientists believe the grayish-blue coloring on the first several inches prevents sunburn as they pull leaves off tree branches. The length is also more impressive than a giraffe's tongue. Okapi tongues can range from 14-18 inches on their smaller frame, while a huge giraffe only has a 20-inch tongue!

35. OKAPI

Dark in color with bright, white stripes . . . it's not a zebra but an okapi! At first glance, you might think okapi and zebras are genetically associated, but okapis are actually related to giraffes. Both are even-toed mammals with prehensile tongues, and the males' share their horn-like ossicones. Shy creatures, okapis tend to keep to themselves and don't appear openly. If seen, they are generally by themselves, only coming together for reproductive purposes. They are exclusively found in the rainforests of Congo where they grow to over five feet tall and almost eight feet long. With only about 22,000 okapis left in the world, they are considered an endangered species.

BY THE NUMBERS

1	*average litter size*
2008	*the year the first picture was taken of an okapi in the wild*
100	*the approximate number of okapis that live in zoos worldwide*

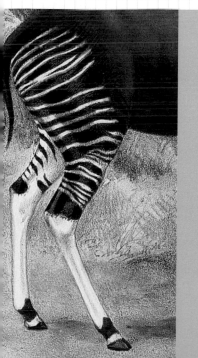

SIGHTLINES

Stripes of the okapi serve as a survival adaptation. They can be referred to as "follow me" stripes because they are believed to help baby okapis track and follow their mothers through the dense rainforest vegetation.

ABOUT THE AUTHOR

Christin is the author of several books for kids, including many in the Little Library of Natural History. She lives with her family in California, where she enjoys rollerblading, puzzles, and a good book.

BUSHEL
& PECK
BOOKS

ABOUT THE PUBLISHER

Bushel & Peck Books is a children's publishing house with a special mission. Through our Book-for-Book Promise™, we donate one book to kids in need for every book we sell. Our beautiful books are given to kids through schools, libraries, local neighborhoods, shelters, nonprofits, and also to many selfless organizations who are working hard to make a difference. So thank you for purchasing this book! Because of you, another book will find itself in the hands of a child who needs it most.